200 YEARS
OF ROCHESTER
ARCHITECTURE AND
GARDENS

200 YEARS OF ROCHESTER ARCHITECTURE AND GARDENS

PHOTOGRAPHY BY ANDY OLENICK

TEXT BY RICHARD O. REISEM
DESIGN BY BILL BUCKETT

The
Landmark Society
of Western New York

Published by the
Landmark Society of Western New York
with support from the
New York State Council on the Arts

Second Printing, 1996
First published in the
United States of America in 1994
by the Landmark Society of
Western New York, Rochester, NY
14608-2204

© 1994 Photographs Andy Olenick

© 1994 Text Richard O. Reisem

Library of Congress Catalog Card
Number: 94-77817
ISBN: 0-9641706-1-2

CONTENTS

*"Architecture is an art
for all men to learn, because
all are concerned with it."*

John Ruskin, 1853

Printed in the USA
by Canfield & Tack Inc.
Rochester, NY 14608-2802

CHAPTER I

ELEGANT BEGINNINGS

1792-1842

PAGE 11

CHAPTER II

VICTORIAN EXUBERANCE

1843-1897

PAGE 37

CHAPTER III

MASTERFUL REVIVALS

1893-1937

PAGE 83

CHAPTER IV

NEW DIRECTIONS

1936-1994

PAGE 129

INTRODUCTION

In the late 1700s much of the area that now constitutes the city of Rochester was considered uninhabitable by American pioneers. Bears and wolves prowled the hills and valleys of the heavily forested glacial terrain. Rattlesnakes slithered through tangled mats of high alders, choke cherries, and high-bush huckleberries. The marshes bred fever-bearing mosquitoes. Through this forbidding wilderness ran the mighty Genesee River, which in a series of cataracts within the current city limits dropped 260 feet before emptying into Lake Ontario. The main falls alone was 96 feet high. In the days before electricity, the power potential of this portion of the river was so vast that it caused pioneers to overcome their reluctance to settle here. Ebenezer Allan was the first settler at the Genesee Falls, and his architectural contribution consisted of two ramshackle mills. In July 1788, he contracted with Oliver Phelps, owner of the land, to erect saw and grist mills at the falls. Allan built the sawmill in 1789. The first lumber sawed there was used to put a roof on the mill. Then came the lumber for Allan's grist mill. The third use for lumber from Allan's mill was for a house to be built by Orringh Stone, who came from Lennox, Massachusetts, in 1790.

Stone first built what is now the rear section of his house, which still stands at 2370 East Avenue as a Landmark Society museum, in post-and-plank construction with clapboards covering exterior walls. The Stone family moved into this trim and sturdy home in 1792, and being on the main route from Canandaigua and Pittsford to the Genesee Falls, it became a tavern. Reputedly, many famous people drank Stone's applejack and native whiskey and were housed there on their travels through this region. These guests included Aaron Burr, Lafayette, Joseph Brant (the Mohawk chieftain), and most famous of all, Louis Philippe, later King of France.

Louis Philippe arrived in 1797 with his two brothers, the Duke of Montpensier and Count Beaujolais, to see this new world of Indians and wilderness and particularly the spectacular waterfalls on the Genesee River. Their arrival was the cause for the first royal dinner in these parts, and it occurred at Orringh Stone's house. An Indian runner had been sent ahead to warn Mrs. Stone, who turned out a feast that included roast pig, wild pigeon, turkey, cornbread, apple and pumpkin pies, plus, of course, plenty of Orringh Stone's applejack and whiskey.

Years later, Louis Philippe was reminded of his Genesee Country expedition when he observed an especially immense and grand plate-glass window being shipped from Paris. Louis Philippe inquired who had ordered such an elegant piece of glass and learned it was destined for the facade of C. F. True's dry goods store in downtown Rochester, New York. He exclaimed incredulously, "What can they do with that in that awful mudhole?"

What Louis Philippe didn't know was that years before that incident, Abelard Reynolds had placed even fancier plate glass from Paris in the curving entrance of the Reynolds Arcade, and that was part of an 1840 renovation of his arcade building that was originally erected in 1828, at which time it was the largest and most expensive building in the United States west of Albany and the finest in the state outside of New York City. The Erie Canal had come to Rochester in 1823 and transformed it into America's first boomtown, so Rochester did not remain a mudhole for long after Louis Philippe's visit.

Samuel Andrews built a stone house at the corner of Main and St. Paul Streets in 1815; Hervey Ely and John G. Bond planted sugar maples on the west side of Washington Street for decoration and shade in 1816, and Charles J. Hill built the first brick house on South Fitzhugh Street in 1821.

The first settlers in Genesee Country built in the Federal style, the kind of architecture they grew up with in New England. Later settlers, those who moved west in the 1820s and later, carried with them — like Bibles — carpenter's manuals that taught them to build a new style of house, Greek Revival. These buildings symbolized the wish to live as freshly and vibrantly as the ancient Greeks whom they admired. They even bestowed on their cities, towns, and hamlets names from the land of Greece. Consider the following in upstate New York: Troy, Ithaca, Palmyra, Ionia, Sparta, Attica, Macedon, Artistotle, and not to forget Rochester's contiguous suburb, Greece.

Greek Revival architecture had symmetry and stateliness as exemplified by the 1837 Hervey Ely House. These buildings looked like Greek temples with columns, porticos, and often triangular pediments, such as seen on the Jonathan Child House, also 1837. The exterior stucco found on these two houses is very special and was expensive to add over the brick or stone construction underneath. The secret of its excellent composition was known only to the French craftsman who was brought here from New York City to apply it. Unfortunately, he died suddenly taking his secret with him.

Both the Ely and Child houses are situated in Rochester's first residential neighborhood, the Third Ward, now called Corn Hill. At various times in the past, it was also dubbed the "Ruffled Shirt District" or the "Silk Stocking District," reflecting the many impressive houses and the upper middle-class owners who lived in them. On this gentle hill where it was once thought that the Seneca Indians raised corn, the wealthy millers and merchants built their mansions alongside workers' cottages. It was an era before sweeping lawns became an essential element of a wealthy estate, so Corn Hill is a compact area of closely spaced dwellings. And since everyone could easily walk to work a few blocks away in the mills, offices, and shops, only the richest homeowners maintained horses and carriages on their limited properties. Corn Hill continued to develop until the end of the 19th century with varied architectural styles including Greek Revival (1830-1860), Gothic Revival (1840-1880), Italianate (1840-1880), Second Empire (1860-1890), and Queen Anne (1870-1900). It became a city preservation district in 1972.

The next upper-class residential area to develop was Rochester's most beautiful street, East Avenue, three miles of grand and graceful mansions. At its peak in the late 1920s, the avenue had almost 100 fabulous houses in diverse and eclectic styles. Josiah Bissell, the great Erie Canal engineer who built one of the mansions on East Avenue, gave the street its name. Early on, it was called the Road to Pittsford. Then it was called Main Street because it was sort of an extension that veered off Main Street at the present Liberty Pole. Bissell petitioned the Rochester common council to change the name to East Avenue. But when they took no action, he did. He wrote later, "I named East Avenue by fastening a number of signs painted with that name upon every street corner of the avenue." The city didn't take down the signs nor did they ever officially accept the name. East Avenue just grew on everybody.

The early East Avenue mansions were built on substantial estates. Joseph Hall built a racetrack on his estate to demonstrate the speed of his spirited horses. In 1865, he sold the track to James Vick who converted it to a seed nursery, but evidence of the track remains today in the curve in Park Avenue between the two straightaways of the former track, Vick Park A and Vick Park B. Near his East Avenue mansion, H. H. Warner, the patent medicine king, built an observatory (since demolished) 31 feet in diameter, which had a dome on the third floor mounted on a track that permitted the huge telescope to be rotated to any point in the sky.

The charming Gothic Revival house that Josiah Bissell built was at 666 East Avenue. Its Gothic design is attributed to the famous local architect Andrew Jackson Warner, but in 1852 when the house was built, Warner was 19 years old, so it is unsure how helpful he could have been at that age. The house was constructed from stone salvaged from the first Erie Canal aqueduct downtown. That aqueduct had to be replaced because the Medina sandstone, which had been quarried from a site in the Genesee River gorge about where Holy Sepulchre Cemetery is located today, was so porous that the aqueduct leaked badly. If the stone leaked at the aqueduct, it seems reasonable that it would also leak in the walls of the house. That thought occurred to Josiah Bissell, so he had a sheet of lead installed as a blanket in all of the walls to keep the house damp-proof.

Of course, the grandest of East Avenue mansions is the George Eastman House, a Georgian Revival stately home completed in 1905 and since 1969, a National Historic Landmark. One example in the design of the George Eastman House indicates how seriously many homeowners regarded the architecture of their dwellings. Eastman started planning his house in 1902. He bought 10 acres on East Avenue, looked at houses in America and England, drew up innumerable rough plans, had Kodak's Camera Works make up a 4 x 6-foot scale model, photographed the model from every angle, and when it seemed that every refinement was made, he enlisted the services of local architect J. Foster Warner and the firm of McKim, Mead & White of New York City as consultants. Warner's design contained 37 rooms, 12 bathrooms, 9 fireplaces, and a large music room, 30 feet square and two stories high. It was impressive enough, yet the music room bothered Eastman for years. Finally, in 1919 he made a dramatic alteration. "I found my music room was too nearly square," he said, "so I decided to cut the house apart and move the rear part, weighing 2500 tons, back 9 feet, 4 inches, adding one space or bay to the room. It took 5 or 6 weeks to cut the house in two and jack it up on rollers, but only 7 hours to move it. Even the architect thought I was foolish, but he told me this morning he had received a lesson in architectural proportions." Sumptuous entertaining on the avenue reached its zenith in Eastman's era.

East Avenue became a city preservation district in 1969. Of the eight preservation districts in the city, those represented in this book include East Avenue, Third Ward, Mount Hope, Grove Place, Susan B. Anthony, and Brown's Race.

The oldest building in downtown Rochester is St. Luke's Episcopal Church, a very early example of Gothic Revival architecture. It was built in 1824, a year after the Erie Canal was completed to Rochester, and stood immediately adjacent to the canal (now Broad Street). Today, downtown Rochester embraces a panorama of historic and contemporary styles, including the very eccentric. The Powers Building falls in the latter category. For many years in the late 1800s, Daniel Powers worked determinedly to have the tallest building in town. The original design in 1869 by Andrew Jackson Warner stopped at a mansard roof. When other buildings around him were built higher, Powers added a second tier of mansard roof and the beginnings of a tower. Again, others built higher still, so Powers added more floors to the tower and a third tier of mansard roof giving a wedding-cake look to this famous city landmark. The Powers Building is one of 73 city landmarks in Rochester at this time. Most of these landmarks appear on the following pages.

Unlike many cities in America, Rochester is younger than some of its suburbs. Pittsford, for example, was well established when the first village settlement occurred in 1812 at what is now known as Four Corners in downtown Rochester. Outstanding early architectural examples from these nearby suburbs, such as Pittsford, are included in this book.

Charles Sprague Sargent, the first director of Harvard University's Arnold Arboretum, called Rochester "a city in a forest." It is an apt description because the area was originally a forest of red, black, and white oaks; chestnuts; hickories; black walnuts; beeches; red and sugar maples; basswoods; tulip trees, and white ashes. Even after many trees were cut to clear land for building, replanting occurred to decorate and shade city streets and lawns. Josiah Bissell was responsible for planting the first street trees on both sides of East Avenue. They were horse chestnuts. Some people contend that the horses that were hitched to the trees died from eating the bark of the horse chestnuts. Others maintain that the horse chestnuts died from the horses eating the bark. Perhaps both are true. In any case, the horse chestnuts had to be replaced with elms, which now, too, are gone.

When George Ellwanger came to America from Germany in 1835 to open a nursery business in Tiffin, Ohio, the packet boat that carried him westward on the Erie Canal made a stopover in Rochester. It was a long-enough stay for young Ellwanger to determine that Rochester had an ideal climate and particularly suitable soil for horticulture. He went on to Tiffin anyway, but he couldn't get Rochester out of his mind, and he came back to open his nursery here with Patrick Barry as a partner. Their nursery grew to 650 acres on the city's south side and became the largest such operation in the world. With many other nurseries also operating here, Rochester became and still is "The Flower City."

Frederick Law Olmsted, the renowned landscape architect, designed the major Rochester parks — Genesee Valley Park, Highland Park, Maplewood Park, and Seneca Park. He also designed a parkway system for Rochester. Today, Lakeview Park and Seneca Parkway most closely reflect his original plan. Rochester was the last municipal park system designed by the great Olmsted, considered the father of American landscape architecture. His work in Rochester also includes smaller areas, such as Plymouth Circle, Schiller Park, and Washington Square. After the senior Olmsted retired, his firm continued to do work in Rochester, designing Brown Square, Cobb's Hill Park, Jones Square, Susan B. Anthony Park, and the University of Rochester Quadrangle. In Genesee Valley Park alone, Olmsted planted 70,000 trees. And there are nearly the same number of street trees in the city. Such a verdant environment of indigenous flora, extensive nurseries, and masterfully designed parks had a profound effect on Rochester's population. The city's many beautiful public and private gardens attest to that influence.

CHAPTER I

ELEGANT BEGINNINGS 1792-1842

"The surest test of the civilization of a people is to be found in their architecture, which presents so noble a field for the display of the grand and the beautiful, and which at the same time is so intimately connected with the essential comforts of life."—William H. Prescott, Historian (1847).

Rochester passed Prescott's test of civilization very early. The first settlers constructed crude, simple log cabins, but they quickly graduated to more sophisticated architecture. When the first sawmills were established at the falls on the Genesee River, finished lumber became available, and the architecture that the settlers remembered from their New England background sprouted here. Raw materials were also plentiful. One of the early settlers, Hamlet Scrantom, wrote in 1812, "The country is very pleasant and fertile, timbered with oak, chestnut, hickory, black walnut, and white wood, some of enormous size. I saw one white-wood log 12 feet long which produced 1000 feet of clapboards."

The lumber was soon put to elegant use. Since the Federal style was predominant in New England at the time, it was in this light and delicate style that early Rochesterians built. Federal style had its roots in neoclassical architecture in England, best exemplified by the Adam style named for the two architect brothers who made it popular. The eldest and most talented brother, Robert Adam, was particularly successful in making his architectural designs the ruling style in England from 1760 to 1780.

But after the War of 1812, American taste turned against British fashions. The Federal style now seemed too delicate and refined for this young, vibrant country. Americans wanted a style of their own, and for inspiration, they turned to the Greeks, whose democratic principles they admired. Greek Revival became the fresh, dynamic style of the early 19th century. It was robust and heroic, yet elegant and symmetrical, eminently suited to the image that Americans had of their civilization.

LEFT & ABOVE: Oliver Culver walked from Vermont to Genesee Country in 1789. He came to trap beaver and muskrat. In his early days here, he killed a 400-pound bear with his hunting knife. However unlikely it seems, Culver built this elegant and disciplined Federal-style house in 1816 when other settlers were constructing crude log houses. Its quiet, symmetrical features, especially the slender columns and delicate cornices of the entrance, seem antithetical to the rough, brawling lives of pioneers.

ABOVE & RIGHT: The rear portion of the Orringh Stone House was built in 1792 at the intersection of two Seneca Indian trails. It was the custom of early settlers to receive guests, and Stone's house, strategically located on such principal routes, became a famous tavern and inn. The front addition, in more refined Federal style with wooden quoins at the corners, was built in 1805. Today it is a house museum of the Landmark Society.

LEFT: *The Erie Canal not only carried flour from Rochester to eastern markets, it was also a principal means of transportation for people, who wanted taverns along the way. Richardson's Canal House was built in 1818, restored in 1979, and is a popular restaurant today, whether guests arrive by boat or other means. It retains most of its original Federal-style architectural details and is the oldest Erie Canal tavern surviving in its original form and still on canal water.*

ABOVE: *Christmas decorations in the canal house.*

ABOVE RIGHT: *The Oliver Loud Inn, built in 1812, is now a bed-and-breakfast in Richardson's Canal Village.*

RIGHT: *The Marquis de Lafayette, Governor DeWitt Clinton, Commodore Cornelius Vanderbilt, and Franklin D. Roosevelt were among the guests at the Phoenix Hotel (circa 1812), during its 125-year history as a stagecoach inn and hotel in Pittsford. The predominant architectural style at that time was Federal. The Phoenix Hotel, now owned by Wolfe Publications, exemplifies the style with an elliptical fanlight over the door and windows set in symmetrical rows.*

LEFT: *The oldest surviving public building in Rochester is St. Luke's Episcopal Church built in 1824, a rare early example of Gothic Revival architecture with pointed-arch windows and fragile tracery in the tower. It was designed by New York City architect Josiah R. Brady. Next to it, the Rochester Free Academy Building (1872-1873), which was Rochester's only public high school for 30 years, is representative of late 19th-century High Victorian Gothic.*

ABOVE: *The U.S. Government under President Thomas Jefferson established the port of Charlotte in 1805, and in 1822 the first lighthouse erected on the shores of Lake Ontario was built here. It is a 40-foot stone tower with 4-foot-thick walls and a winding wrought-iron staircase. The lamp used was visible for 20 miles. This museum is also a city landmark and on the National Register of Historic Places.*

PREVIOUS PAGES: *Tulips in Highland Park.*

ABOVE LEFT: *The Thomas Weddle family arrived in Rochester more than 150 years ago and built this Corn Hill house. Weddle was in the paint business. Corn Hill is a compatible mixture of middle-class homes like this one, mansions, and workmen's cottages. They were all built with good materials, fine craftsmanship, and classical details.*

LEFT: *The Henry Shaw House is a city landmark in the Third Ward (Corn Hill) Preservation District. Shaw, a fur trader, built it for his parents and sister who arrived from England in 1837. It reflects the simplicity and careful proportions of an urban Greek Revival house.*

RIGHT & ABOVE: *Rochester is the center for cobblestone architecture, a western New York construction technique of building sturdy structures from small stones laid in horizontal rows. Most of them were built in the Greek Revival style. One exception is this 1830 Federal-style James Tinker House built of small, field cobblestones.*

LEFT: *This Federal-style house now located in Pittsford, dates to circa 1832. Originally built in Marion, New York, by a Quaker family from Rhode Island, the house shows the disciplined craftsmanship of early carpenters in precise woodworking inside and out. The house was an important station on the Underground Railroad before the Civil War. A cleverly disguised wood-storage closet beside a fireplace concealed as many as 8 or 9 escaping slaves when slavehunters came around.*

RIGHT: *From the top down: kitchen, library, and guest bedroom.*

LEFT: *Benjamin Campbell quickly built a fortune milling flour at the Genesee Falls. In 1835 he spent a good part of it to build a handsome Greek Revival house, but six years later when the price of flour plummeted, he was bankrupt, and his house was sold at public auction. Frederick Whittlesey acquired it in 1852, and his family occupied the house until the need to preserve it led to the founding of the Landmark Society, which acquired it in 1937 and made it into the city's first house museum. The double parlors show the carefully restored original paint colors.*

ABOVE: *The entrance is on the side of the house.*

LEFT & ABOVE: *The highly successful merchant and banker Jonathan Child built his splendid Greek Revival mansion in 1837 from designs by the famous Boston architect S. P. Hastings. At the time, local citizens thought the house to be so grand and sumptuous that they called it "Child's Folly." Child had other views that differed from those of the populace: As Rochester's first mayor, his refusal to sign liquor licenses demanded by the pioneer community led to his resignation.*

RIGHT: *On warm summer evenings, the Hervey Elys often entertained their Livingston Park neighbors on their elegant Greek Revival piazza. S.P. Hastings chose Doric columns for Ely's house; the Child house has more detailed Corinthian columns. From this 1837 Corn Hill home, Hervey Ely walked to work every day at the largest, most automated flour mill in town. But even high productivity did not save him from financial disaster and the loss of his handsome house when the price of flour plummeted.*

RIGHT: Between 1838 and 1841, the wealthy dry goods merchant Silas O. Smith built one of the most distinguished Greek Revival houses in upstate New York on his 95 acres of wooded land on what is now East Avenue. The round turret atop a square belvedere is a unique feature by the architect/builder, Alfred A. Badger. Today, Woodside is home to the Rochester Historical Society.

ABOVE LEFT: The enclosed garden.

LEFT: The rear porch.

Left & Previous Pages: The Elihu Kirby House, built in 1840, was moved in 1956 from Henrietta to its present Pittsford site. In order to move it, the house had to be cut in half and moved in two separate, 50-ton sections. It took 10 days for the rear section to travel the 3 1/2 miles because it got bogged down in mud. Fletcher Steele, the nationally famous Rochester landscape architect, designed the gardens. When Steele died, Katharine Wilson Rahn completed the design. The west facade appears on the previous two pages; the double parlors are at left.

Clockwise from Above Left: Entrance to part of the five-acre gardens, the front facade, the apple orchard, and the Fletcher Steele allée looking toward the north facade.

LEFT: Fire destroyed the 1816 Triphammer Building in 1977, but revealed deep in the basement the massive, 25-foot-diameter, wood-and-iron water wheel that powered the two huge hammers used to forge wrought-iron tools, such as scythes.

ABOVE LEFT: In the foreground is the 1873 Rochester Water Works Holly pump station, which provided water at particularly high pressures to fight downtown fires as taller and taller buildings were constructed. Today, the building houses the Center at High Falls with historic exhibits concerning flour-milling days when waterpower attracted the first industry in Rochester.

ABOVE RIGHT: In order to continue its route westward to Buffalo, the Erie Canal had to cross the Genesee River on an aqueduct. Canal engineers decided to accomplish the prodigious feat in downtown Rochester. The first attempt in 1823 leaked and crumbled, so a second aqueduct was completed in 1842, which with a 45-foot-wide waterway allowed two-way traffic. Today, an upper deck accommodates vehicular and pedestrian traffic. The 1881 statue of Mercury stands above the Lawyers Cooperative Publishing Company. In the background is the 1977 First Federal Plaza tower.

CHAPTER II

VICTORIAN EXUBERANCE 1843-1897

LEFT & ABOVE: The 35-room Wilson Soule House, designed in Richardsonian Romanesque style by local architect J. Foster Warner in 1892. The house was later owned by George Eastman and today provides offices for Asbury First United Methodist Church.

In the Victorian period, it can be said, architecture gained height. High ceilings, tall windows, and emphasis on vertical proportions were common features of most architectural styles of the period, especially Gothic Revival, Italianate, and Second Empire. Also, there was a reaction to the order and symmetry of Federal and Greek Revival styles in enthusiasm for asymmetry, rambling floor plans, combinations of facing materials, forms from different historic sources in western civilization, and variety of color in exterior facades.

Although the Wilson Soule House at 1050 East Avenue was built at the end of the Victorian period when styles had become quieter and more homogeneous, the way the house came about was very much in the flamboyant spirit of the Victorian age. Soule was 37 years old when his father died in 1890, leaving Wilson an estate of $2 million and the highly successful Hop Bitters Patent Medicine Company. Weeks after his inheritance, Soule hired the most prominent architect in town, J. Foster Warner, to design a proper home for a man of his newly acquired wealth. His only instruction to Warner was that there be eight bedrooms on the second floor. He said there were no restrictions regarding expense, and he gave Warner power of attorney over his multimillion-dollar bank account. He then said that he and his family were going abroad for two years and wanted the house to be completed by his return.

Warner was not hesitant in spending Soule's money. He chose to design the house in the Richardsonian Romanesque style and to use only natural materials, no man-made ones — or "artificial materials" as he called them — in the basic fabric of the house. There was to be, therefore, no brick, tile, terra cotta, cement, or concrete. The principal building material was the best Indiana limestone he could find. The house that Warner designed had 35 rooms on three floors, plus an enormous attic that formed a fourth floor. The basement not only covered the entire area underneath the house but extended under the porches as well. It was so vast that Warner installed a shooting gallery in the basement. The style of the reception room was Indo-Persian, finished in India teakwood elaborately and delicately carved by craftsmen in India. The ceiling was gold filigree. The drawing room was Louis XVI, the library, Byzantine, and the dining room, Elizabethan. One of the stone sidewalk slabs that Warner ordered in Oxford bluestone was 8'-3" x 17'-4". It was so large and heavy that no existing railroad car could carry it, and a special flat car had to be built to transport it to Rochester. It was all definitely Victorian exuberance.

LEFT: Ornate curves and carvings on the entrance to the 1849 Henry A. Brewster House look as if they should belong to a Turkish palace, but they add an exotic touch to a basically Italianate design by local architect Mervin Austin and reflect the Victorian taste for novel forms.

RIGHT & BELOW: The Charles F. Bissell House was built in 1852 with Medina sandstone salvaged from the first Erie Canal aqueduct constructed in 1823.

LEFT: Besides distinguishing himself as a physician and the talented builder of his 1853 Gothic Revival house in Pittsford, Dr. Hartwell Carver was the father of the transcontinental railroad and helped drive the golden spike that connected the east and west by rail. Union Pacific gave him a triumphant tour over the railroad to California in 1871. His house is distinguished by steep gables, elaborate barge boards, and board-and-batten siding.

ABOVE TOP: The William E. Arnold Tract was laid out in 1853 with a mall down the center of the street to give Arnold Park some of the distinction of East Avenue. Elaborate stone posts were added in 1888 at the entrances on East and Park Avenues.

ABOVE: Unlike its more grandiose neighbors on nearby East Avenue, this 1875 Second Empire house was designed with a Pullman-style plan to fit on a long, narrow lot, 40 by 150 feet. The first-floor rooms, therefore, and four out of the five bedrooms tucked under the mansard roof have southern exposure.

ABOVE: In the middle and latter 1800s, the Ellwanger & Barry Nursery with its 650 acres on Mount Hope Avenue was the largest operation of its kind in the world. Their charming Gothic Revival office with its crenellated tower and triple-flue chimney, was designed by the preeminent American architect of the period, Alexander Jackson Davis, and built in 1854.

LEFT: In 1854, bank president, court judge, and newspaper publisher Horatio Gates Warner fulfilled his desire for the remote in time and place by designing a 22-room house reminiscent of a Scottish castle of his mother's Clan Douglas. The thick walls are made of hand-hewn gray stone. Doors are thick, too; the 62 doors in the house are all 2 1/2 inches thick.

PREVIOUS PAGES: When Patrick Barry, who was a partner with George Ellwanger in the world's largest nursery in the 19th century, wanted a residence to suit his position, he turned to the prominent English architect Gervase Wheeler for its design. Wheeler provided this splendid 16-room mansion in Italian Villa style. The house was built from 1855 to 1857.

LEFT & ABOVE: The University of Rochester acquired the Barry property in 1962 and painstakingly restored the house to its Victorian splendor and richness. Ceilings in this grand house are 13 feet high, and doors, which are grained to imitate rosewood or mahogany, are 11 feet.

LEFT: The graceful entrance-hall staircase.

CLOCKWISE FROM TOP LEFT: the dining room, a window detail, the front parlor, and the garden with a perennial border leading to the carriage house.

ABOVE: *Colonel Thomas C. Bates, a canal forwarder and railroad contractor, built this Italian Villa house in 1856. Thomas Leighton, president of a bridge-building firm, acquired it in the late 1870s and by adding a wing made it the largest mansion on East Avenue at the time. Thomas B. Ryder of Sibley, Lindsay & Curr Company bought it in 1910 and enlarged it further. The four Ryder children were thrilled when moving in to find a pony in one of the barn stalls and a new pony cart beside it.*

ABOVE RIGHT: *A rear porch faces south for maximum sun.*

BELOW: An old gnarled yew tree, imported from Japan soon after Admiral Perry opened trade in 1863, was the inspiration for the Japanese garden created in 1990 at the Bates-Ryder House by one of the condominium owners.

ABOVE: Lumber merchant Emmet Hollister decided on a brick house for himself. The Hollisters moved into their new home designed to resemble an Italian villa (shown on the left in the photograph) in 1864. Another Civil War house went up to the right of the Hollisters in 1865. Here there is French influence, specifically Second Empire. It appears no larger than its neighbor, although there is an extra floor of living space and illustrates how a mansard roof reduces apparent height and mass.

BELOW: The Susan B. Anthony House (1866) is one of two National Historic Landmarks in Rochester. (The other is the George Eastman House.) Anthony led America's women's rights movement in the late 1800s and early 1900s. She and her fellow suffragists drafted many of their documents including the 19th Amendment to the U.S. Constitution in the third-floor room shown below. The Anthony Amendment became law in 1920.

ABOVE: *When Samuel Hildreth constructed his Pittsford farmhouse in 1814, he built it in the Federal style. The house has had a colorful history. It was a stop on the Underground Railroad. One owner, Frank Hawley, specialized in shady deals and mysteriously disappeared in 1898. But the biggest event in the house's history was its complete conversion to the Italianate style in the 1860s when popular taste also caused many other Pittsford houses to be Italianized.*

PREVIOUS PAGES: *In 1867, the great Rochester horticulturist George Ellwanger created a perennial garden adjacent to his Mount Hope Avenue home, which stood across the street from his famous nursery. The garden design is based on English natural gardens popular at the time. Particularly outstanding are the old peonies visible along with hosta and irises on the previous two pages.*

ABOVE & LEFT: Housing construction in Rochester boomed after the Civil War. Even the venerable Ellwanger & Barry Nursery on Mount Hope Avenue decided to enter the real estate market by erecting houses on some of their nursery land. Here is one of four adjacent Victorian houses they built in 1868. With 2600 square feet of living space, it was advertised for sale at $5000.

FOLLOWING PAGES: Historic colors accent the details of the Jacob S. Irwin House in Corn Hill. Irwin built his spacious Second Empire home in 1872. When his daughter beat him at a Sunday afternoon game of croquet, the eccentric Irwin disinherited her. She got the house anyway when her father left it to her children.

ABOVE: The Daniel Powers Building grew in layers starting with the first mansard roof in 1869. When others built taller buildings around him, Powers asked his architect, Andrew Jackson Warner, to keep adding floors and a tower in order to stay above the crowd. The first elevator in Rochester was installed in this building with hydraulic power provided by the Holly Pump Station of the Rochester Water Works in Brown's Race.

LEFT: The Powers Building is elegantly appointed on the interior with a cast-iron staircase and black-and-white marble floors, all recently meticulously restored.

FOLLOWING PAGES: The elaborate decorative treatment on the Main Street facade.

ABOVE: *The High Victorian Gothic gate-house in Mount Hope Cemetery with its squat columns, arches, and high-pitched roof was designed by Andrew Jackson Warner and built in 1874. When the cemetery offices were moved south, the building became the headquarters for the Friends of Mount Hope Cemetery.*

RIGHT: Rochester provided 5000 men to the Union Army in the Civil War. The city was also a treatment center for wounded soldiers. The Civil War plot in Mount Hope Cemetery includes a poignant bronze sculpture of a company bugle boy and a weary soldier carrying the Union flag. The sculpture was created by Sally James Farnham, a noted American artist who worked with the great Frederick Remington.

BELOW: When Henry Searle designed this Gothic Revival chapel after studying Gothic Revival buildings throughout the country, he boasted that "we are to have something at Mount Hope which will excel in everything but outlay of money anything of the kind in the United States." And indeed the 1862 building stands out, partly because of J. Foster Warner's 1912 crematory addition with a smokestack that even Warner's great design skill could not disguise.

ABOVE: *This massive Romanesque Revival building designed by Andrew Jackson Warner served as Rochester's City Hall for 103 years from 1875 to 1978. There is a 6,230-pound bell, Rochester's Big Ben, in the square tower, but the commercial offices that now occupy the building have little reason to ring it.*

ABOVE: *The prolific Rochester architect Andrew Jackson Warner drew plans for a small (40 feet by 70 feet) but graceful chapel built in 1876 over a crypt for the tombs of Rochester's Catholic bishops in Holy Sepulchre Cemetery. Medina sandstone quarried from the banks of the Genesee River a few blocks away and a steep slate roof were combined to create an Early English Gothic structure. The separate chapel tower was added in 1886.*

RIGHT: *A cemetery entrance gate detail.*

LEFT: In the Grove Place Preservation District downtown are the eclectic Tudor Revival townhouses built in 1878 by Theodore Bacon as a row of six, three-story units for members of his family. One year before the townhouses were built, George B. Selden invented the gasoline automobile in his uncle's barn directly behind the site.

ABOVE LEFT: This brick Queen Anne house was built in 1881 with fanciful embellishments, such as carved gargoyle consoles on the front corners of the second floor, decorative porch railings, and finials at the ends of the roof peaks. All of it is meticulously cared for today by the Zen Center.

ABOVE RIGHT: Behind the house, the Zen Buddhists have constructed a Japanese garden.

ABOVE: *Rochester architect John R. Thomas designed this charming brick house with stone-arched windows and prominent corner turret, a feature of the Chateauesque style. Built in 1879, this was a wedding house for William W. Chapin, son of the early Rochester pioneer, Louis Chapin, and William's bride, Elizabeth Lyon.*

ABOVE: *This romantic Victorian house was a wedding present from William Cogswell to his eldest daughter, Martha, in 1878. Cogswell also hired local architect John R. Thomas to design the house. Here is High Victorian Gothic with five different window shapes (three shapes on the front facade), steep gables, finials, and ornamental ribs and brackets.*

LEFT & ABOVE: Hulbert Harrington Warner used his marketing skills and a patented formula for a mixture of alcohol, water, sugar, and a few herbal flavorings to make a fortune selling patent medi-cines. The fortune permitted him in 1882-1883 to build this factory with a cast-iron facade. In its prime, the factory turned out 7000 gallons of "medicine" a day.

ABOVE: *The great promise of young local architect and designer Harvey Ellis is evident in this 1883 Queen Anne house. It invited the colors and forms of outdoor nature inside through a myriad of windows. It was exactly what Alexander B. Lamberton, a founder of the Rochester park system, wanted to achieve in his home.*

LEFT & ABOVE: *In 1882, the U.S. Congress authorized $300,000 to build a federal building in Rochester. The supervising architect in the Treasury Department was 36-year-old Mifflin Bell, and many say that this Richardsonian Romanesque structure was his best work. Others attribute the design to Harvey Ellis. In any case, by 1886, the masonry work was completed to the second story. Government had infinite wisdom in those days as well. Congress decided to authorize an additional $200,000 for a bigger building, so plans had to be redesigned and a larger building started. In 1978, the building was renovated to become Rochester's City Hall. The spectacular atrium is a dramatic setting for frequent public events.*

BELOW: *Magnolias have bloomed every spring on the Oxford Street mall since 1880 when H. E. Hooker, owner of Hooker Brothers Nursery, designed the street. The magnolias, a hybrid cross between a Chinese white and a Japanese purple, are noted for their delicate color.*

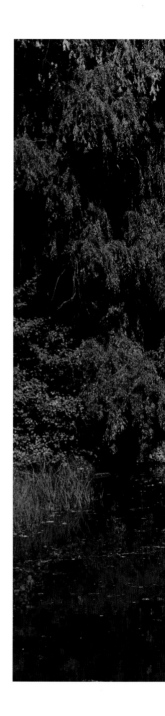

ABOVE & RIGHT: There is just cause for calling this Queen Anne structure "The Sunflower House." A sunflower motif is repeated on the exterior as well as interior, and the principal color of the house is bright yellow. A master carpenter, William Parr, built the house in 1887-1888.

Above: *Genesee Valley Park was developed from 1889 to 1903. The great designer of New York City's Central Park, Frederick Law Olmsted, also designed this rolling, pastoral Rochester park, which surrounds the confluence of the Genesee River and the Erie Canal, as well as Red Creek shown above. His design called for planting 10,500 shrubs and nearly 70,000 trees.*

ABOVE: *The Genesee River provided power to run 19th-century industrial equipment, so the hub of all early industrial activity was the river, and buildings were constructed to its very edge. The Ellis Building in the foreground is a seven-story Romanesque Revival structure designed by Harvey Ellis in the late 1800s. Even utilitarian structures often received decorative treatment; note the clusters of triple windows and rounded arches on the fifth floor. Ellis also incorporated varied materials: pressed brick, cut Medina sandstone, wrought iron, and terra cotta.*

LEFT: *Elisha Johnson, principal landowner on the east side of the Genesee River, made a bold attempt in 1817 to get the proposed county courthouse built on his side of the river by giving the city a central square named for George Washington. But Col. Rochester won the courthouse for the west side. Washington Square remained undeveloped until 1892 when the city finally decided to erect a memorial to soldiers who served in the Civil War. The monument is topped by a bronze statue of Abraham Lincoln. Below him are figures representing infantry, cavalry, artillery, and marine.*

BELOW: *An infantry soldier stands guard before the 30-story Xerox Building.*

LEFT & ABOVE: *The 1893 imposing Victorian Gothic landmark, St. Bernard's Seminary, was designed by Andrew Jackson Warner. Founded by Bishop Bernard McQuaid, it had enrollments, sometimes as high as 250 students, for 88 years before closing in 1981. For the construction, Warner proposed using red Medina stone quarried from the Genesee River gorge nearby. Bishop McQuaid was warned that parts of this stone were very soft and cautioned against its use, but McQuaid replied, "I have never seen a stone that would not hold up in its own climate."*

LEFT & ABOVE: *The distinguished English architect Robert Gibson designed the Gothic-style Christ Church on East Avenue with construction beginning in 1892. The church, of Albion sandstone, incorporated the sanctuary and a portion of the nave of the original 1855 church to serve as a chapel. Stained-glass windows, altar mosaics, and the sanctuary mosaic pavement depicted at left are outstanding works from the Tiffany Company.*

RIGHT: *Heins & LaFarge, the architects who designed the still unfinished Cathedral of St. John the Divine in New York City, also designed St. Paul's Church on East Avenue. The Gothic Revival church opened in 1897. George Eastman, although not a regular member, contributed to the building fund and attended services, occasionally placing a tightly rolled $50 bill in the collection plate.*

CHAPTER III

MASTERFUL REVIVALS 1893-1937

After the flamboyance of the Victorians, public taste returned to simplicity and order, so architects revived the formal classicism of styles culled from the past. One example of this traditionalism was the Beaux Arts style, named for the school that taught and promoted it, the Ecole des Beaux Arts in Paris. The Granite Building at the corner of Main and St. Paul Streets is a handsome, somewhat subdued example of the style. It was designed by J. Foster Warner and built in 1893-1894 in cream-colored brick and the granite that gives the building its name. With steel-frame construction, the first in Rochester, floors of heavy tile, and a cast-iron staircase, the 12-story structure was proudly proclaimed fireproof. The building received the ultimate test of this at 5 a.m., February 26, 1904, when a 5-cent fuse blew in the electrical system operating the elevators of the Rochester Dry Goods Company located several doors to the east of the Granite Building. When the fuse blew, it spat out bits of red-hot molten metal that landed in a stack of draperies. The fire burned for 40 continuous hours and totally destroyed most of the block, despite the combined efforts of the Rochester, Buffalo, and Syracuse fire departments. It completely gutted the Granite Building, but the shell remained standing — the only building in the fire to do so. J. Foster Warner's office was on the 11th floor. He lost all of his plans for the new store that Sibley's intended to build at Clinton and Main, plus the drawings for the George Eastman mansion and the new West High School.

In the midst of all the masterful revivals — such as Beaux Arts and including inspiration from such diverse sources as Italian Renaissance architecture; Jacobean, Georgian, and Gothic styles in England; Norman design in France; Lombardy Romanesque; Greek Temple, and Byzantine — came a number of architects who developed new styles of ornamentation and started a trend toward modernism. Here were architectural approaches that did not relate to historical forms — the naturalistic and stylized foliage of Arts and Crafts, the chevrons and zigzags of Art Deco, and the long, low, Prairie style of Frank Lloyd Wright.

LEFT & ABOVE: The Granite Building was designed by J. Foster Warner and built in 1893-1894. Fireproof construction saved it from total destruction in a catastrophic 1904 fire.

ABOVE: *The Monroe County Office Building was formerly the county courthouse, the third courthouse built on this site. The first was completed in 1822; a larger one was built in 1851, and this elegant building designed by J. Foster Warner in Italian Renaissance Revival style (the first example of this style in western New York) was constructed from 1894 to 1896. An 8-foot, gold-painted, wooden statue of Justice, which was originally atop the dome of the second courthouse on the site, stands in a niche on the fourth floor above the entrance.*

RIGHT: *The opulent interior of the Monroe County Office Building has a center atrium with Italian marble walls; four different styles of columns; several types of Italian marble on floors, stairs, doorframes, and columns; Cuban mahogany; intricate designs in brass, copper, and iron; and elaborate friezes.*

ABOVE & RIGHT: In 1903, James Sibley Watson hired New York architect John du Fais to design a library wing for his house on Prince Street. As inspiration, du Fais used the Petit Trianon, the summer palace of Marie Antoinette at Versailles. When the main house was razed in the 1950s, the library wing was spared and is a private residence today.

FOLLOWING PAGES: The ceiling of the Watson library has carved wooden gargoyles, hunting dogs, and rows of exotic painted animals all attributed to the Rochester architect and artist Harvey Ellis.

BELOW TOP: *The west garden was designed by Claude Bragdon in 1916 based on a Lutyens-Jekyll garden at Hestercombe House in England.*

BOTTOM: *The west facade overlooks the formal garden and its central armillary, which has symbolic representations of celestial spheres.*

ABOVE: *The 35,000-square-foot, Georgian Revival George Eastman House, designed by J. Foster Warner and McKim, Mead & White, was under construction from 1902 to 1905. It has 37 rooms plus 13 baths and 9 fireplaces. It cost $300,000 to build but $1.7 million to restore in 1989-1990. The largest single-family residence ever built in Monroe County, the house was declared a National Historic Landmark in 1969.*

ABOVE: *In the billiard room, there is a raised platform at the far end of the room for onlookers to sit and watch the game.*

RIGHT ABOVE: *The walls of the living room are covered in silk damask; the corner ceiling medallions recently restored in carved plaster represent the four seasons. Most of the furniture in the room is original, including the chandelier.*

RIGHT BELOW: *George Eastman liked to have breakfast in his conservatory while his private organist, Harold Gleason, played favorite selections on a giant Aeolian pipe organ.*

Left: At an elevation of 640 feet, the gate-house at Cobb's Hill provides an excellent view of the city beyond. The 1908 Greek temple was designed by J. Foster Warner. Olmsted Brothers designed the city park around it.

Left Below: This station, with its unusual Norman Chateau tower, was built in 1905 by Lehigh Valley Railroad, which was one of several railroads that ran through Rochester in earlier days. The building extends over the Genesee River on wide iron girders supported by 40-foot stone piers. Service to the station was discontinued in 1955.

Far Right: When the First Universalist Church was placed on the National Register of Historic Places, the U.S. Department of Interior expressed the opinion that "it is one of the finest pieces of architecture in the State," and they ranked it in importance with Trinity Church in Boston. The 1908 church, designed in the Lombardy Romanesque style, represents the best qualities of Claude Bragdon's work.

Right: Bragdon's stained-glass windows in the lobby describe the Gospels. An ox represents Luke who wrote about the sacrificial ox, and a lion stands for Mark and the ministry of Christ.

PREVIOUS PAGES: *Early in his career, Frank Lloyd Wright designed 120 Prairie-style houses (about 90 survive) with long, low horizontal lines intended to blend in with the flat land of the midwest prairies. The dining room of his easternmost Prairie house has furniture designed by Wright. Built in 1908, the house has 220 leaded-glass windows with more than 4000 individual pieces of glass in the dining room alone.*

BELOW: *After the great fire of 1904 destroyed their old store, Sibley's opened a new one, designed by J. Foster Warner, in 1905. The new store dwarfed most department stores in the country, starting with 5 acres and growing to 13 acres of floor space by 1911. Here is the eye-catching clock tower.*

ABOVE: *Unquestionably the most handsome factory in Rochester is the Gleason Works. The Pan-American Building in Washington, D.C., was the inspiration for this imposing neoclassical facade built in 1910. Inside, Gleason makes the machinery to cut or grind gears.*

RIGHT: *THIS 1899 statue of Frederick Douglass, the first statue of a black man to be erected in the U.S., stood for many years at the intersection of St. Paul Street and Central Avenue. Susan B. Anthony complained that Douglass would never have approved of his statue facing south. This was corrected in 1941 when the statue was moved to Highland Park where it now faces north.*

LEFT: As Rochester's wealthiest person until George Eastman, Hiram Sibley, founder of Western Union, lived comfortably in his 30-room mansion on East Avenue. The house was built in 1868 as an Italianate structure complete with a cupola and tall Victorian windows. But in 1912 when tastes changed, a later generation of Sibley's family extensively remodeled the house in Colonial Revival style seen here.

ABOVE: The former living room in the Hiram Sibley House is the board room for offices today. With more than 18,000 square feet, the house is a spacious and elegant setting for commercial use.

ABOVE: *Emily Sibley Watson gave the original 1913 Memorial Art Gallery building to the University of Rochester in memory of her son from her first marriage, James G. Averell, a young architect who died of cholera at the age of 26. Just a few months before his death in 1904, Averell sketched the Malatesta Temple in Rimini, Italy, so Mrs. Watson's nephew-in-law, John Gade, a New York architect, designed the original gallery building after Averell's favorite Italian temple.*

LEFT & ABOVE: Additions to the Memorial Art Gallery were made in 1925, 1968, and 1987. The latest, designed by Frank S. Grosso, tied the gallery to the Cutler Union. James Goold Cutler – architect, inventor of the Cutler Mail Chute, and University of Rochester trustee, – mentioned at a Prince Street Campus banquet in the early 1900s that "I should like to see some day on this campus a noble building, with a fine tower and a large hall suitable for such dinners as this – something like the great hall of Christ Church College in Oxford. After I am gone, you may find some provision for realizing such a desire." His large bequest paid for this grand Collegiate Gothic building, built in 1932-1933.

LEFT: The nationally famous local land-scape architect Fletcher Steele designed this walled town garden in 1926 for Charlotte Whitney Allen. In her day, a Gaston Lachaise marble statue of a woman was the focal point at the end of the garden. Today, that sculpted nude stays warm inside the Memorial Art Gallery.

RIGHT: Alling DeForest, another famous local landscape architect, designed this walled private city garden in 1932.

ABOVE: *In 1922 Rochester architect
Herbert Stern designed a house for his
parents in the English Regency style.
With its refined simplicity and tastefully
executed details, it is the quintessence of
an elegant city house.*

RIGHT: *City gardens become complemen-
tary settings for architecture and also in
this scene, screening from the street for
an East Avenue house.*

LEFT: Hiram Sibley, Jr., built the Hiram Sibley Building in 1925 and named it for his famous father, founder of Western Union. The superbly detailed 20th-Century Georgian building was designed by Shepley, Bulfinch & Abbott of Boston.

RIGHT & BELOW: The Rochester Community Savings Bank on Franklin Street is an architectural gem designed in 1928 by McKim, Mead & White of New York City with local architect J. Foster Warner. The exterior of this "Temple of Commerce" is of Kato stone quarried in Minnesota.

FOLLOWING PAGES: With columns of rouge royal marble, teller counters of sienna marble, and floors of marble mosaic, the interior of the Rochester Community Savings Bank is a luxurious, 20th-century interpretation of the Byzantine style. Below the inscription, "Industry and Thrift are the Foundations of Prosperity," there is an elaborate mosaic painting by the famous muralist Ezra Augustus Winter, who depicted a winged woman, Prosperity, rewarding Industry, a seated man surrounded by agricultural tools and produce, and Thrift, a woman holding a child and a treasure chest.

111

ABOVE: George Eastman built one of the most beautiful and largest theaters in the U.S. in 1922 and donated it to the University of Rochester "for the enrichment of community life." The theater, designed by McKim, Mead & White, is elegant and dignified in every aspect, except perhaps for two washtub chandeliers. When a need for light fixtures in the far top balcony was determined too late for the grand opening, a worker gilded and hung a pair of metal washtubs, which are still there.

RIGHT: Twelve wallpaper panels in the Eastman Theatre lobby celebrate the ancient Greek myth of Psyche's love for Cupid. The original woodblocks were commissioned by Napoleon Bonaparte in 1814 from which the panels were printed in 50 shades of gray. The lobby panels were replaced in 1971 with the last set of prints available from the only reprinting, which was made in 1923.

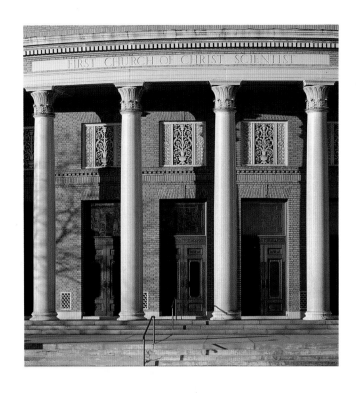

LEFT: Marble and granite were considered fitting materials to express the strength, sincerity, and stability of a bank. Classical design was also important. The one-story First National Bank, designed by Mowbray and Uffinger of New York, is 72 feet high, also appropriately impressive for 1924.

RIGHT: In 1916, the First Church of Christ Scientist erected a handsome edifice designed by Edwin S. Gordon. When the architect's original plan in the Romanesque style was rejected by the church, the architect changed the design dramatically by preparing drawings for an Italian Renaissance church with four majestic columns on the front facade.

BELOW: The Rundel Memorial Library, built from 1933 to 1936 with classical moderne Art Deco details, sits on pilings in the old Johnson-Seymour Raceway. In fact, water still runs in the raceway under the library and empties into the river through spillways beneath the building. The American Institute of Architects considered it one of the seven most important architectural works in New York State built between 1931 and 1961.

ABOVE: This Pittsford house was reconstructed in Colonial Revival style after fire destroyed an earlier house. Francis Mitchell rebuilt the house in 1922 from plans by Gordon and Kaelber, and although he was a bachelor, Mitchell included many bedrooms with individual bathrooms, plus six bedrooms for his five Swedish servants and one Japanese butler.

RIGHT: Redbud trees and forsythia bloom along Mitchell Road in Pittsford.

ABOVE: *Ward Wellington Ward (1875-1932) was a talented Syracuse architect who designed 38 houses in greater Rochester. Most of his work was in the Arts and Crafts style like this Brighton house built in 1923. In his houses, Ward incorporated the work of many craftsmen using Mercer tiles to decorate fireplaces and stained-glass windows with naturalistic figures.*

LEFT: *Local architect Carl Schmidt was working for the firm of Gordon and Kaelber in 1930 when he first designed the Medical Arts Building in a style that was then in declining popularity — Classical Revival. His colleagues kidded him about being ignorant of the new modern style, Art Deco. Schmidt replied that any fool could design in Art Deco and drew up a second set of plans in the new style. To Schmidt's surprise, the client, when shown both plans, chose the Art Deco design.*

BELOW: *Just before the 1929 crash, local architect Edgar Phillips designed the Little Theatre (300-seat capacity) in the Art Deco style with a facade of black terra cotta..*

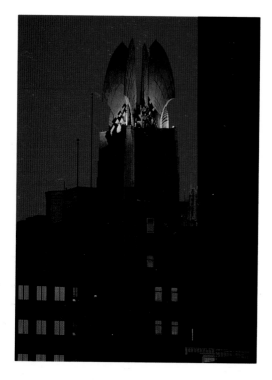

ABOVE: *Topped with four aluminum wings, each 42 feet high and weighing 7500 pounds, the Times Square Building is the most eccentric Art Deco building in town. These "Wings of Progress" were the inspiration of New York architect Ralph T. Walker who said the idea came to him on a Florida beach when he set four seashells on end and found they suggested "a sense of flight, a sense of upward lift." But the building has remained firmly grounded since it was built in 1930 with its cornerstone laid on the same day as the 1929 stock market crash.*

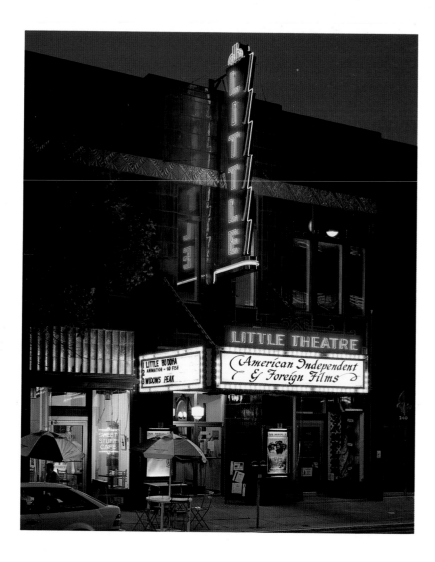

LEFT: *On the question of style for the new campus of the University of Rochester, President Rush Rhees said, "We must have a development that will be architecturally worthy and academically suitable." Local architects Edward Gordon and William Kaelber interpreted that in the mid 1920s as a revival of the American past, chiefly Greek Revival. A few Renaissance touches were included to give added majesty to the dome of the library in the celebrated university quadrangle.*

RIGHT: *Monroe Community Hospital (1930) is covered with terra cotta gargoyles, heads, and intricate architectural details. These delightful touches and the rest of the 20th-century Italianate design are the work of Siegmund Firestone, a native of Romania who received his education in Germany, and finally moved his architectural practice from New York City to Rochester. The black architect, Thomas W. Boyde, obtained his start in Rochester in his early twenties working on the design of this building. When Boyde applied for the job, Firestone's secretary announced with a distinct lack of enthusiasm that there was a young black man in the office who maintained he was an architect. But Firestone was charmed and impressed by Boyde, and he joined the firm that designed a hospital far advanced for its time.*

ABOVE: The Ontario Beach Park Carousel, built in 1905, is one of the oldest merry-go-rounds in the country and was designed by the premier carousel builder Gustav Dentzel. Riders have a view of Lake Ontario as they revolve on Dentzel's menagerie of 52 carved animals, including cats, rabbits, ostriches, pigs, donkeys, a tiger, a lion, a deer, a goat, and lots of horses.

PREVIOUS PAGES: On the crest of an esker left by glaciers 14,000 years ago stand the 1931 English Gothic brick structures of the Colgate Rochester Divinity School. The buildings were designed by New York City architect James Gamble Rogers whose distinguished work includes many buildings on the campus of Yale University. Unlike traditional denominational seminaries, Colgate Rochester prepares students from all communions for the ministry.

ABOVE & RIGHT: Architect Joseph P. Flynn designed the Rochester Fire Department headquarters on Andrews Street with its stylized Art Deco carvings of firemen at the entrance. The two buildings that make up the headquarters were built from 1935 to 1937.

CHAPTER IV

NEW DIRECTIONS 1936-1994

*I*n 1936 Gustave Fassin, a Kodak scientist, designed and built a house for himself in a wooded section of Irondequoit. Fassin, who worked in lens manufacturing at Kodak's Hawk-Eye Plant, acquired rejected glass lenses from Kodak and incorporated them in the interior of his house as others would use glass brick to transmit light through floors and walls. There was a singular absence of ornament on the exterior; the house had a flat roof, smooth and uniform concrete wall surfaces painted white, horizontal bands of windows that turned around corners, a small circular window here and there, and a sleek triple band of metal for a roof cornice. It was modern, and since the inspiration came from Europe with practitioners like Walter Gropius and Ludwig Mies van der Rohe in Germany, J. J. P. Oud in Holland, and LeCorbusier in France, it was known as the International style. Its debut in Rochester in the Fassin house was a highly noted event, and the interior won Fassin the local Lillian Fairchild Award in 1936.

Rochester, with its great stock of traditional architecture, began to embrace contemporary styles, such as seen in the First Unitarian Church, the new Henrietta campus of the Rochester Institute of Technology, and the University of Rochester's Wilson Commons. For the Strasenburgh Planetarium, local architect Carl F. Kaelber, Jr., sculpted in concrete the dynamic, curved forms reminiscent of a spiral nebula. Another local architect, James H. Johnson, broke completely with historical association in designing the Mushroom House, which although it was built more than two decades ago still looks visionary.

A number of notable American architects have contributed their considerable talents to Rochester's contemporary architectural scene, including Louis I. Kahn (First Unitarian Church), Pietro Belluschi (Temple B'rith Kodesh), Welton Beckett (Xerox Building), Kevin Roche and John Dinkeloo (Rochester Institute of Technology), I. M. Pei (University of Rochester Wilson Commons), James Stewart Polshek (Rochester Riverside Convention Center), Herbert Newman (Eastman School of Music Living Center), Hellmuth/Obata/Kassabaum (Clinton Square Building), and Fox and Fowle (Bausch & Lomb Building).

LEFT & ABOVE: The International-style Gustave Fassin House (1936) is distinguished by smooth concrete walls, a flat roof, horizontal bands of windows that wrap around corners, and glass brick.

BELOW: Four towers at the corners of the sanctuary bring natural light into the central room of the First Unitarian Church designed by the internationally renowned architect Louis I. Kahn. Built in 1962, the church includes a 1969 addition also designed by Kahn. In the school rooms that surround the sanctuary, the windows are set in deep brick reveals to prevent glaring light from entering.

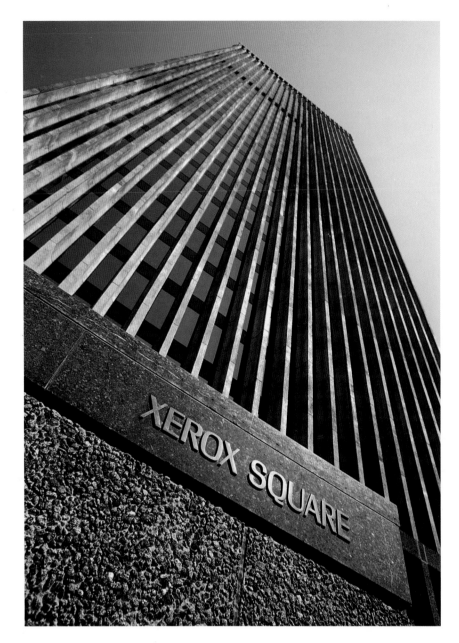

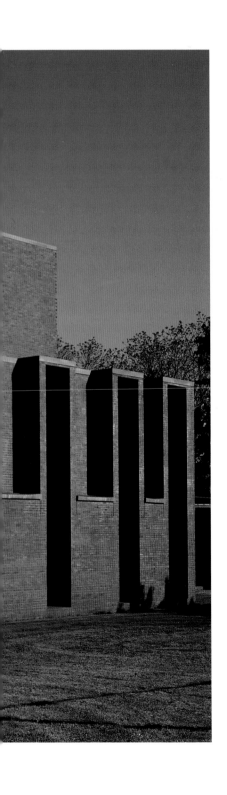

ABOVE: The tallest building in Rochester is the 30-story, 440-foot Xerox Tower, designed by Welton Beckett & Associates and built in 1967. Xerox Corporation joins Eastman Kodak Company, Bausch & Lomb Inc., and over 90 other optics and imaging firms to position Rochester as "The World's Image Centre." Rochester has a larger percentage of highly skilled people in its work force than almost any other metropolitan area in the country. The city is one of the top ten exporting cities in the U.S. with over 40 percent of New York State's total exports.

LEFT: *All stainless steel and Formica, the Highland Park Diner on South Clinton Avenue is fascinating Art Moderne from the 1940s. Inside, it is still time for meatloaf and mashed potatoes with gravy, finished off with a chocolate shake served not in a paper cup but in a real soda-fountain glass and topped with whipped cream and shaved chocolate.*

ABOVE: *Each of the twelve panels of the 65-foot-high dome on Temple B'rith Kodesh represents one of the twelve tribes of Israel. The temple was designed by west coast architect Pietro Belluschi and dedicated in 1963. Established in 1849, B'rith Kodesh is one of the oldest active synagogues in the country.*

RIGHT: *With more than 15,000 students, the Rochester Institute of Technology is the largest university in the area. It is also the oldest, dating back to 1829. Since 1968, the school has occupied a sprawling 1300-acre suburban campus in Henrietta. Seven million identical face bricks were laid in the 13-building complex of the main campus. Kevin Roche and John Dinkeloo designed the administration building depicted here.*

BELOW: The famous local landscape architect Alling DeForest designed this private urban garden – an open lawn ringed by green plants and entered through a decorative wooden arch.

BOTTOM: This urban garden off East Avenue is attractively terraced to accommodate the slope of the small rear yard. The owner and designer of the garden is the nationally renowned Rochester sculptor Albert Paley.

ABOVE & RIGHT: It's hard to believe that this house, popularly called the Mushroom House, was built in 1971. The owners wanted an imaginative, contemporary look in a single-level structure. The steep hills and ravine on the site didn't lend themselves to a single level, so local architect James H. Johnson devised a stem-and-pod design, inspired by Queen Anne's lace growing wild on the site, to stand over the ravine and blend with the landscape.

FOLLOWING PAGES: The organic approach continues inside the Mushroom House with tree-like forms rising and branching out from the center of the five pods, each of which is 30 feet in diameter.

BELOW: *Designed by Carl F. Kaelber, Jr., in the shape of a spiral galaxy, the Strasenburgh Planetarium of the Rochester Museum and Science Center was considered to be the most modern and well equipped planetarium in the world when it opened in 1968.*

BOTTOM: *The Strong Museum was constructed in 1982 to house the collection of Victoriana of Margaret Woodbury Strong. Her collection includes 22,000 dolls and 600 fully furnished doll houses, but the museum today has a broad focus on American life in the 19th and 20th centuries. The building was designed by John Ungar and Northrop, Kaelber & Kopf.*

RIGHT: *"There is nothing more static and oppressive than large, monumental windowless space," said architect I. M. Pei. He ensured that didn't occur in the University of Rochester's Wilson Commons by including a dramatic glass atrium in his 1976 design.*

RIGHT: *The Eastman School of Music Living Center was added to the downtown Rochester skyline in 1990. The Post Modern building was designed by Herbert Newman and houses students of the music school a block away.*

BELOW: *James Stewart Polshek, the dean of Columbia University's School of Architecture and the prominent New York City architect who designed the Rochester Riverside Convention Center, called it "the best building I've ever done; it really is glorious." When another architect saw the plans for the convention center, he concluded that "Polshek was into rectangles." Polshek replied, "No, I'm into grids." The Post Modern building, under construction from 1982 to 1985, is $40 million of elegant grids.*

OPPOSITE PAGE: *The latest addition to Rochester's downtown skyline is the Bausch & Lomb Building, completed in 1995. Designed by Fox & Fowle Architects of New York City with Handler Grosso Durfee Bridges Architects, Rochester, the granite-clad building includes a glass-enclosed winter garden facing Washington Square and a 65-foot-high steel sculpture by local artist Albert Paley in the entrance circle to the left. The building under construction is an addition to the central library. Visible to the right are edges of the Post Modern 1990 Clinton Square Building and behind it the vertical, white piers of the 1973 Chase Plaza Tower. In the background are the First Federal Plaza Tower with its circular top floor and Eastman Kodak Company world headquarters.*

140

INDEX

Adam style 11
Adam, Robert 11
Aeolian pipe organ 92
Albion sandstone 81
Allan, Ebenezer 6
Allen, Charlotte Whitney 107
America's first boomtown 7
American Institute of Architects 117
Andrews Street 127
Andrews, Samuel 7
Anthony, Susan B. 51, 100
armillary 92
Arnold Arboretum 9
Arnold Park entrance 41
Art Deco style 83, 117, 120, 121, 127
Art Moderne style 133
Arts and Crafts style 83, 90, 118, 119
Asbury First United Methodist Church 37
Austin, Mervin 39
automobile, invention of 67
Averell, James G. 104
Bacon, Theodore 67
Badger, Alfred A. 28
Barry, Patrick 9, 47
Bates, Col. Thomas C. 48
Bausch & Lomb Building 129, 140, 141
Bausch & Lomb Inc. 131
Beaujolais, Count 6
Beaux Arts style 82, 83
Beckett, Welton 129
Bell, Mifflin 73
Belluschi, Pietro 129, 133
Bevier Memorial Building 90, 91
Big Ben, Rochester's 64
Bissell, Josiah 7, 9
Bond, John G. 7
Boyde, Thomas W., Jr. 122
Brady, Josiah R. 19
Bragdon, Claude 90, 92, 96
Brant, Joseph 6
Brighton 118
British fashions 11
Broad Street 8
Broad Street Bridge 35
Brown Square 9
Brown's Race 59
Brown's Race Preservation District 8
Buell, George C. 90
Burr, Aaron 6
Byzantine decoration 37
Byzantine style 83, 111
Campbell, Benjamin 25
Campbell-Whittlesey House 24, 25
carousel, Ontario Beach Park 126
Carver, Dr. Hartwell 41
cast-iron facade 70
Center at High Falls 35
Chapin, Louis 68
Chapin, William W. 68
Chapin-Rosenberg House 68
Charles E. Hart House 50, 51
Charles F. Bissell House 8, 39
Charlotte Lighthouse 19
Charlotte, port of 19
Chase Plaza Tower 140, 141
Chateauesque style 68
Child, Jonathan 7, 27
Christ Church 80, 81
Christ Church College, Oxford 104
City Hall, New 72, 73
City Hall, Old 64

city landmark 9, 20
Civil War 63, 77
Classical Revival style 121
classical moderne 117
Clinton Square Building 129, 140, 141
Clinton, Governor DeWitt 15
Cobb's Hill gatehouse 96
Cobb's Hill Park 9
Cobblestone architecture 21
Cogswell, Martha 68
Cogswell, William 68
Colgate Rochester Divinity School 124, 125, 126
Collegiate Gothic style 104, 105
Colonial Revival style 102, 103, 118
Columbia University School of Architecture 140
Corinthian columns 26, 27
Corn Hill 7, 21, 27, 54
County courthouse 84
crematory, Mount Hope Cemetery 63
Cro Nest 90
Cuban mahogany 85
Culver, Oliver 11
Cutler Mail Chute 104
Cutler Union 104, 105
Cutler, James Goold 104
Daniel Powers Building 2, 8, 58, 59, 60, 61
Davis, Alexander Jackson 43
DeForest, Alling 107, 134
Dentzel, Gustav 126
Dinkeloo, John 129, 133
Doric columns 27
Douglass, Frederick 100, 101
duFais, John 86
Early English Gothic style 65
East Avenue 7, 8, 28, 41, 103, 108, 134
East Avenue Preservation District 8
Eastman Kodak Company 131, 140, 141
Eastman School of Music Living Center 129, 140
Eastman Theatre 114, 115
Eastman, George 8, 37, 81, 83, 92, 103, 114
Ecole des Beaux Arts 83
elevator, first in Rochester 59
Elihu Kirby House 30, 31, 32, 33
Elizabethan decoration 37
Ellis Building 76
Ellis East 71
Ellis, Harvey 71, 73, 76, 86
Ellwanger & Barry Nursery 54, 55
Ellwanger & Barry Nursery Office 43
Ellwanger Garden 52, 53, 54
Ellwanger, George 9, 47, 54
Ely, Hervey 7, 27
Emmet Hollister House 50
English Gothic Revival style 8, 124, 125, 126
English natural garden 52, 53, 54
English Regency Revival style 108
Erie Canal 7, 8, 9, 15, 35, 75
Erie Canal aqueduct 8, 35
Erie Canal sandstone 39
Farnham, Sally James 63
Fassin, Gustave 129
father of transcontinental railroad 41
Federal style 7, 10, 11, 13, 14, 15, 21, 22, 23, 37, 54
Fire Department Headquarters 127
Firestone, Siegmund 122

First Church of Christ Scientist 117
First Federal Plaza tower 35, 140, 141
First National Bank 116, 117
First Unitarian Church 129, 130, 131
First Universalist Church 96, 97
Flower City 9
Flynn, Joseph P. 127
Formica 132
forsythia 118
Four Corners 9
Fox and Fowle 129
Franklin Street 111
Friends of Mount Hope Cemetery 62
Gade, John 104
gargoyles 122
Gatehouse, Mount Hope Cemetery 62, 63
Genesee Falls 6
Genesee River 6, 8, 35, 75, 76, 77, 79, 96
Genesee Valley Park 9, 75
George C. Buell House 90
George Eastman House 8, 92, 93, 94, 95
George Eastman Theatre 114, 115
George Washington Square 77
Georgian Revival style 8, 83, 92, 93, 110, 111
Gibbs Street townhouses 66, 67
Gibson, Robert 81
Gleason Works 100, 101
Gleason, Harold 92
Gordon and Kaelber 118, 121
Gordon, Edward 122
Gordon, Edwin S. 117
Gothic Revival style 7, 8, 11, 18, 19, 37, 40, 41, 43, 63, 65, 68, 69, 78, 79, 80, 81, 83, 104, 105, 124, 125, 126
Granite Building 82, 83
Greek Revival style 7, 11, 20, 21, 24, 25, 26, 27, 28, 29, 37, 122
Greek Temple style 83, 96
Gropius, Walter 129
Grosso, Frank S. 104
Grove Place Preservation District 8, 67
Gustave Fassin House 128, 129
H. H. Warner Building 70
Hall, Joseph 8
Hastings, S. P. 27
Hawley, Frank 54
Heins & LaFarge 81
Hellmuth/Obata/Kassabaum 129
Henrietta 129, 133
Henry A. Brewster House 38, 39
Henry Shaw House 20
Herbert Stern House 108
Hervey Ely House 7, 27
Hestercombe House 92
High Victorian Gothic style 18, 19, 62, 63, 68, 69
Highland Park 9, 16, 17, 100, 101
Highland Park Diner 132
Hildreth, Samuel 54
Hill, Charles J. 7
Hiram Sibley Building 110, 111
Hiram Sibley House 102, 103
Hollister, Emmet 50
Holly Pump Station 35, 59
Holy Sepulchre Cemetery 8, 65
Holy Sepulchre Cemetery Chapel 65
Hooker Brothers Nursery 73
Hooker, H. E. 73

Hop Bitters Patent Medicine Co. 37
horse chestnuts on East Avenue 9
Indo-Persian decoration 37
International style 128, 129
Irving Place 64
Irwin, Jacob S. 54
Italian marble 85
Italian Renaissance Revival style 83, 84, 90, 91, 117, 122
Italian Villa style 44, 45, 46, 47, 48, 49, 50
Italianate style 7, 37, 38, 39, 54, 103, 122, 123
Jacob Irwin House 54, 56, 57
Jacobean Revival style 83, 90
James Sibley Watson Library 86, 87, 88, 89
Japanese garden 49, 67
Jefferson, President Thomas 19
Johnson, Elisha 77
Johnson, James H. 129, 134
Johnson-Seymour Raceway 117
Jonathan Child House 7, 26, 27
Jones Square 9
Justice, statue of 84
Kaelber, Carl F., Jr. 129, 138
Kaelber, William 122
Kahn, Louis I. 129, 130
Kato stone 111
Kodak Camera Works 8
Kodak Hawk-Eye Plant 129
Lachaise, Gaston 107
Lafayette, Marquis de 6, 15
Lake Ontario 6
Lakeview Park 9
Lamberton, Alexander B. 71
Landmark Society 6, 12, 25
Lawyers Cooperative Publishing Company 35
LeCorbusier 129
Lehigh Valley Railroad Station 96
Leighton, Thomas 48
Liberty Pole 7
Lillian Fairchild Award 129
Lincoln, Abraham 77
Little Theatre 121
Livingston Park 27
Lombardy Romanesque style 83, 96, 97
Louis Philippe 6
Louis XVI decoration 37
Luke, the apostle, 96
Lyon, Elizabeth 68
magnolias 73
Malatesta Temple, Rimini 104
mansard roof 9, 41, 50, 51, 59
Maplewood Park 9
Margaret Woodbury Strong Museum 138
Marie Antoinette 86
Marion, NY 23
Mark, the apostle 96
McKim, Mead & White 8, 92, 111, 114
McQuaid, Bishop Bernard 79
Medical Arts Building 120, 121
Medina sandstone 8, 39, 65, 76, 79
Memorial Art Gallery 104, 105, 107
Mercer tiles 118
Mercury, statue of 35
merry-go-round 126
Mies van der Rohe, Ludwig 129
Mitchell Road 118
Mitchell, Francis 118

Monroe Community Hospital 122, 123
Monroe County Courthouse 84, 85
Monroe County Office Building 84, 85
Montpensier, Duke of 6
Mount Hope Avenue 43, 54, 55
Mount Hope Cemetery 62, 63
Mount Hope Preservation District 8
Mowbray and Uffinger 117
Mushroom House 129, 134, 135, 136, 137
Napoleon Bonaparte 114
National Historic Landmark 51, 92
National Register of Historic Places 96
Neoclassical style 100
New City Hall 72, 73
Newman, Herbert 129, 140
Norman Chateau style 96
Norman Revival style 83
Northrop, Kaelber & Kopf 138
Old City Hall 64
Old Federal Building 72, 73
Oliver Culver House 10, 11
Oliver Loud Inn 15
Olmsted Brothers 96
Olmsted, Frederick Law 9, 75
Ontario Beach Park Carousel 126
Orringh Stone House 12, 13
Oud, J. J. P. 129
Oxford Street magnolia mall 73
Pan-American Building, Washington, D.C. 100
Park Avenue 8
Parr, William 74
patent medicine 37, 70
Patrick Barry House 44, 45, 46, 47
Pei, I. M. 129, 138
perennial border 47
perennial garden 52, 53, 54
Perry, Admiral 49
Petit Trianon 86
Phelps, Oliver 6
Phillips, Edgar 121
Phoenix Hotel 15
Pittsford 9, 22, 23, 33, 41, 54, 118
Plymouth Circle 9
Polshek, James Stewart 129, 140
Post Modern style 140, 141
post-and-plank construction 6
Powers Building 2, 8, 58, 59, 60, 61
Powers, Daniel 9
Prairie style 83, 98, 99, 100
Prescott, William H. 11
Prince Street Campus, University of Rochester 104, 105
Pullman-style plan 41
Queen Anne style 7, 67, 71, 74
Rahn, Katharine Wilson 33
Red Creek 75
redbud trees 118
Remington, Frederick 63
Reynolds Arcade 7
Reynolds, Abelard 7
Rhees, Rush 122
Richardson's Canal House 14, 15
Richardsonian Romanesque style 36, 37, 73
Riverside Convention Center 129, 140
Roche, Kevin 129, 133
Rochester City Hall 72, 73
Rochester Community Savings Bank 111, 112, 113

Rochester Fire Department Headquarters 127
Rochester Free Academy Building 18, 19
Rochester Historical Society 28
Rochester Institute of Technology 129, 133
Rochester Museum and Science Center 138
Rochester park system 9, 71
Rochester Riverside Convention Center 129, 140
Rochester Water Works pump station 35, 59
Rochester, Col. Nathaniel 77
Rogers, James Gamble 126
Romanesque Revival style 64, 76, 117
Roosevelt, Franklin D. 15
Rundel Memorial Library 117
Rush Rhees Library 122
Ryder, Thomas B. 48
Samuel Hildreth House 54
Sargent, Charles Sprague 9
sawmills on the Genesee 11
Schiller Park 9
Schmidt, Carl 121
Scottish castle 43
Scrantom, Hamlet 11
Searle, Henry 63
Second Empire style 7, 37, 41, 50, 51, 54, 56, 57
Selden, George B. 67
Seneca Indians 2, 7
Seneca Park 9
Seneca Parkway 9
Shaw, Henry 21
Shepley, Bulfinch & Abbott 111
Sibley's 83, 100
Sibley, Hiram 103
Sibley, Hiram, Jr. 111
Sibley, Lindsay & Curr Co. 48, 83, 100
Smith, Silas O. 28
Soule, Wilson 37
South Clinton Avenue 133
spiral galaxy 138
spiral nebula 129
St. Bernard's Seminary 78, 79
St. John the Divine, Cathedral of 81
St. Luke's Episcopal Church 8, 18, 19
St. Paul's Church 81
steel-frame construction, first 83
Steele, Fletcher 33, 107
Stern, Herbert 108
stock market crash, 1929 121
Stone, Orringh 6, 12
Strasenburgh Planetarium 129, 138
Strong Museum 138
Strong, Margaret Woodbury 138
Sunflower House 74
Susan B. Anthony House 51
Susan B. Anthony Park 9
Susan B. Anthony Preservation District 8 synagogue 133
tallest building 131
Temple B'rith Kodesh 129, 133
Temple of Commerce 111, 112, 113
The World's Image Centre 131, 140
Third Ward 7
Third Ward Preservation District 8
Thomas Weddle House 20
Thomas, John R. 68
Tiffany Company 81
Times Square Building 121

Tinker House 21
Trinity Church, Boston 96
Triphammer Forge 34, 35
True, C. F. 6
Tudor Revival style 66, 67
Turkish palace 39
twelve tribes of Israel 133
Twentieth-Century Georgian style 110, 111
U.S. Department of Interior 96
Underground Railroad 23, 54
Ungar, John 138
University of Rochester 47, 104, 114, 122, 129, 140
University of Rochester Quadrangle 9
University of Rochester Wilson Commons 129, 138, 139
Vanderbilt, Commodore Cornelius 15
Versailles 86
Vick Park A 8
Vick Park B 8
Vick, James 8
Vick-Allison House 41
Victorian Gothic style 78, 79
Victorian period 37
Walker, Ralph T. 121
War of 1812 11
Ward, Ward Wellington 118, 119
Warner Castle 42, 43
Warner observatory 8
Warner, Andrew Jackson 9, 59, 62, 64, 65, 79
Warner, Horatio Gates 43
Warner, Hulbert Harrington 8, 70
Warner, J. Foster 8, 37, 63, 83, 84, 92, 96, 100, 111
Washington Square 9, 77, 140
Washington Street shade trees 7
Watson Library 86, 87, 88, 89
Watson, Emily Sibley 104
Watson, James Sibley 86
Weddle, Thomas 21
Welton Beckett & Associates 131
Western Union 103, 111
Wheeler, Gervase 47
Whittlesey, Frederick 25
William Chapin House 68
William Cogswell House 68, 69
William E. Arnold Tract 41
Wilson Commons 129, 138, 139
Wilson Soule House 36, 37
Wings of Progress 121
Winter, Ezra Augustus 111
Wolfe Publications 15
Woodside 28, 29
World's Image Centre 131, 140
Wright, Frank Lloyd 83, 100
Xerox Building 77, 129, 131
Xerox Corporation 131
Yale University 126
Zen Buddhists 67
Zen Center 67

Acknowledgments

Although the names Andy Olenick, Richard Reisem, and Bill Buckett appear on the title page of this book, we had a talented and dedicated group of people and organizations supporting our endeavors. These contributors volunteered their considerable efforts, as we did, to this publishing project for the Landmark Society.

We are indebted to Henry McCartney, executive director of the Landmark Society, for the initial idea to produce this book, for his steadfast encouragement and support throughout the project, and for his leadership in all phases of the book's creation, production, promotion, and marketing. Also, the Society's president, Arlene Wright, has been particularly supportive and helpful with the promotion of the book.

Sherri Olenick, the photographer's wife, was indispensable as an enthusiastic and persevering assistant in the planning and creation of the photography. Edgar Praus graciously accommodated the rush and weekend film-processing requirements of the photographer. And Paul Menaguale, Spectrum Color Lab, generously contributed large color prints for prepublication publicity.

Particularly helpful in providing accurate information for the book's content were Tim O'Connell, city of Rochester employee with a vast knowledge of the city's history, and Elizabeth Schmidt, trustee of the Friends of Mount Hope Cemetery and exceptional history researcher. Architectural historian Jean France not only perfected the title of the book but contributed unstintingly of her immense knowledge to its content. Similarly, architectural historian Houghton Wetherald's wise guidance helped to shape the tone and substance of the book. Karl Kabelac, rare books librarian at the University of Rochester and local history expert, combed the manuscript copy to correct and clarify its contents. Ann Parks and Cynthia Howk of the Landmark Society staff similarly applied their impressive expertise to the text and patiently answered a multitude of questions from the author.

Josef Johns, Jack McKinney, and Karen Wolf, all highly experienced readers with unassailable taste and judgment, not only carefully proofread the text, but added significantly to its appropriateness and clarity.

Assisting Bill Buckett on the book's production were Gary Clark and Laurie Magnon, of Buckett Associates Inc., both of whom worked painstakingly at every detail that a project like this one absolutely requires.

The promotion and marketing team was headed by Bill Edwards, CEO of Light Impressions. His publishing knowledge and generosity in so many ways were essential to this book's success. Similarly, Jeff Pollock, president of Silver Pixel Press, provided particularly helpful advice and guidance.

Flo Paxson, Landmark Society staff, developed a comprehensive publicity and promotion plan that is so necessary for a publishing effort like this. Norma Jean Hildreth, Catherine Rourke, and Cheryl Corsi, also of the Society staff, processed the overwhelming book orders, handled a multitude of details, and answered a huge number of telephone inquiries.

Peter Giblin with a professional background in Kodak marketing, Judie Griffin with broad experience in both the arts and business, James Knauf with a bank trust officer's expertise and wide community knowledge, Patricia Place, community volunteer extraordinary, Judy Sullivan with her creative advertising skills, and Beth Teall with a background in public relations and business, combined their diverse capabilities into a remarkably effective marketing and promotion team. The late Carl Furstenberg came to the Society asking how he could help and did so with dedication before his sudden death in the middle of the project.

Finally, we are beholden to all those wonderful Landmark Society members who trustingly purchased so many books sight unseen. They provided the capital to pay bills along the way. Also, Rochester's business community was singularly supportive, as were the Rochester Chamber of Commerce, the Industrial Management Council, and the Rochester Downtown Development Corporation. The City of Rochester's Link Gallery and the Center at High Falls helpfully sponsored photographic exhibits publicizing the book.

The photographer, author, and designer of *200 Years of Rochester Architecture and Gardens* thank all of these skilled and generous people and organizations for their vital contributions. We deeply appreciate their efforts.

Andy Olenick   *September 1, 1994*
Richard Reisem
Bill Buckett